28 Italian Songs and Arias

of the Seventeenth and Eighteenth Centuries

T0088784

Based on the Editions by Alessandro Parisotti

Edited by Richard Walters

International Phonetic Alphabet, Translations and Recorded Diction Lessons by Martha Gerhart

Piano Accompaniments Recorded by Laura Ward

Companion to
50485629   28 Italian Songs and Arias of the Seventeenth and Eighteenth Centuries: Medium Low Voice, Book Only

ISBN 978-1-4950-5456-3

www.musicsalesclassical.com
www.halleonard.com

DISC ONE

DISC TWO

ALESSANDRO PARISOTTI
AND ARIE ANTICHE

If not for the Ricordi publication *Arie antiche*, the name Alessandro Parisotti (1853-1913) likely would have disappeared from music history. Despite his output as a composer of sacred choral music, it is only *Arie antiche*, in three volumes, for which he is remembered. The Italian musician who collected and edited/realized/arranged then forgotten seventeenth and eighteenth century Italian airs is absent from most sources of music research. Parisotti receives a brief note in *Enciclopedia della musica*. He was born in Rome and lived his entire life there. In 1880 he became secretary of the Accademia di Santa Cecilia, an important Roman center of Italian musical research, activity and education since the seventeenth century. He published a treatise on the physics of acoustics, psychology and esthetics of music in 1911.

Research since the publication of *Arie antiche* has shed new light on the authorship of several arias, noted in the articles in this publication. Even so, credit must be given to Parisotti for finding and choosing songs which have stood the test of time, for creating versions of them that remain beautiful, and for conceiving of a collection that influenced vocal study around the world. Other publications of Baroque Italian songs were released in the late nineteenth century and early to mid-twentieth century, but none had the international impact of *Arie antiche*, or its related Schirmer publications *Anthology of Italian Song of the Seventeenth and Eighteenth Centuries* and *24 Italian Songs and Arias of the Seventeenth and Eighteenth Centuries*.

During the 1870s and '80s, much "modern music" was received with nothing short of vehemence. Composers like Liszt and Wagner, who viewed themselves as writing "music of the future," found themselves greeted with scorn and loathing in some circles. It was in this musical climate that Parisotti compiled a collection of arias from the previous two centuries. In the original preface to *Arie antiche*, Parisotti noted that "music… can readily derive from grand models whatever it may need for the improvement and development of its productions." He acknowledged this as a "paraphrase of the well-known saying of our great modern melodramatist." The towering Italian music figure of the day, Giuseppe Verdi, had made a controversial and widely discussed statement in 1871 that a return to the past would actually be progress.

Parisotti's original preface to *Arie antiche* states:

Since these days the truly new is becoming rarer, I am pleased to see the old resurrected in its place. Composers in the seventeenth and eighteenth centuries wrote music that was enlightened, above all, by structural purity and simplicity, emotion, and a quality of the serenity over the complete piece. The music of today is decidedly the opposite: erratic, jerky and full of violent contrasts.

According to Parisotti, the arias in his collections were "… gleaned from old manuscripts and ancient editions, where they lay in unmerited oblivion. … In transcribing the melodies the utmost care was taken to alter nothing in the originals, and often various manuscripts were consulted to ascertain the elegant and correct form." Of his accompaniments and harmonizations of *basso continuo* he noted, "care was taken to insert nothing out of keeping with the words or character of the compositions, or with the style of the author and his period."

The original credit on the *Arie antiche* collection reads "Raccolte ed elaborate da A. Parisotti" (collected and elaborated by A. Parisotti). His source was generally a vocal melody and a figured bass, though for some selections he used previously published nineteenth century realizations/editions which he credited (later removed), particularly those by François Auguste Gevaert and Carl Banck, whose credits are cited in this edition.

Clearly, late nineteenth century ideas of musical objectivity are different from a current view. The Romanticism of Parisotti's period is inescapably part of the style of his editions. His late nineteenth century approach to Baroque music is in itself historical. Musicology was in its infancy in the nineteenth century, particularly in Italy. A concept of early music performance practice did not exist. Parisotti arranged piano accompaniments to support the forgotten melodies he discovered and edited, making the songs comprehensible in style to singers and audiences of the Italian salon song era. Nationalism was also strong in the years following the creation of the unified Italian republic in 1870, and interest in historical Italian song was part of the temper of the times.

Based on his work on *Arie antiche* and the song "Se tu m'ami," attributed to Pergolesi but now presumed to have been a Parisotti original composition, Parisotti was a very good composer and arranger. His realizations/editions of these Baroque songs sound like the fresh work of an inquisitive young man in love with the arias, the voice, and the piano. His accompaniments were written for a modern pianoforte, and are satisfying on the instrument in a way that a purer, more restrained early music approach to realization is not. Though other points of view, reflecting mid to late twentieth century values of Baroque performance practice, have been made to this music since, Parisotti's versions remain musically convincing on their own terms, and are preferred by many singers and teachers.

Added vocal ornamentation is certainly possible in this music beyond Parisotti's suggestions, and is encouraged if tasteful in style. Further suggested ornamentation was outside the purpose of this edition, a fresh presentation of Parisotti's familiar editions, plus the four songs from *24 Italian Songs and Arias of the Seventeenth and Eighteenth Centuries* not edited by Parisotti.

Research sources for this edition were numerous. John Glenn Paton's enlightening research on these songs and arias deserves mention.

Comments on the original 24 Italian Songs and Arias of the Seventeenth and Eighteenth Centuires

Schirmer originally published *24 Italian Songs and Arias of the Seventeenth and Eighteenth Centuries* in 1948, compiled by Lester Hodges. Most of the contents were assembled from the previously released Schirmer publication *Anthology of Italian Song of the Seventeenth and Eighteenth Centuries*, originally released in 1894. The source for this publication was *Arie antiche*, edited by Alessandro Parisotti, published in three volumes by Ricordi beginning in 1885.

28 Italian Songs and Arias of the Seventeenth and Eighteenth Centuries was originally released in 2008 in two keys, Medium High Voice and Medium Low Voice. These keys matched those used in the Schirmer publication *24 Italian Songs and Arias of the Seventeenth and Eighteenth Centuries*. Upon further reflection, and after input from voice teachers, in 2010 we released editions for High Voice, Medium Voice and Low Voice, transposing the songs to additional keys. Five available keys of this essential material create more practical uses among voice students. The High Voice keys will be useful for the highest and lightest voices. Medium Voice keys will suit many mezzo-sopranos, and some high baritones. The Low Voice keys can be helpful for beginning basses, or the occasional contralto. See the last page of this book for a complete chart comparing the keys used in all five editions: High Voice, Medium High Voice, Medium Voice, Medium Low Voice, Low Voice.

Richard Walters
editor

ABOUT THE ENHANCED CDs

In addition to piano accompaniments playable on both your CD player and computer, these enhanced CDs also includes tempo adjustment and transposition software for computer use only. This software, known as Amazing Slow Downer, was originally created for use in pop music to allow singers and players the freedom to independently adjust both tempo and pitch elements. Because we believe there may be valuable uses for these features in other musical genres, we have included this software as a tool for both the teacher and student. For quick and easy installation instructions of this software, please see below.

In recording a piano accompaniment we necessarily must choose one tempo. Our choice of tempo, phrasing and dynamics is carefully considered. But by the nature of recording, it is only one option. Similar to our choice of tempo, much thought has gone into our choice of key for each song.

However, we encourage you to explore your own interpretive ideas, which may differ from our recordings. This new software feature allows you to adjust the tempo up and down without affecting the pitch. Likewise, Amazing Slow Downer allows you to shift pitch up and down without affecting the tempo. We recommend that these new tempo and pitch adjustment features be used with care and insight.

The audio quality may be somewhat compromised when played through the Amazing Slow Downer. This compromise in quality will not be a factor in playing the CD audio track on a normal CD player or through another audio computer program.

INSTALLATION INSTRUCTIONS:

For Macintosh OS 8, 9 and X:
Load the CD-ROM into your CD-ROM Drive on your computer.
Each computer is set up a little differently. Your computer may automatically open the audio CD portion of this enhanced CD and begin to play it.
To access the CD-ROM features, double-click on the data portion of the CD-ROM (which will have the Hal Leonard icon in red and be named as the book).
Double-click on the "Amazing OS 8 (9 or X)" folder.
Double-click "Amazing Slow Downer"/"Amazing X PA" to run the software from the CD-ROM, or copy this file to your hard disk and run it from there.
Follow the instructions on-screen to get started. The Amazing Slow Downer should display tempo, pitch and mix bars. Click to select your track and adjust pitch or tempo by sliding the appropriate bar to the left or to the right.

For Windows:
Load the CD-ROM into your CD-ROM Drive on your computer.
Each computer is set up a little differently. Your computer may automatically open the audio CD portion of this enhanced CD and begin to play it.
To access the CD-ROM features, click on My Computer then right click on the Drive that you placed the CD in. Click Open. You should then see a folder named "Amazing Slow Downer". Click to open the "Amazing Slow Downer" folder.
Double-click "setup.exe" to install the software from the CD-ROM to your hard disk. Follow the on-screen instructions to complete installation.
Go to "Start," "Programs" and find the "Amazing Slow Downer" folder. Go to that folder and select the "Amazing Slow Downer" software.
Follow the instructions on-screen to get started. The Amazing Slow Downer should display tempo, pitch and mix bars. Click to select your track and adjust pitch or tempo by sliding the appropriate bar to the left or to the right.
Note: On Windows NT, 2000, XP and Vista, the user should be logged in as the "Administrator" to guarantee access to the CD-ROM drive. Please see the help file for further information.

MINIMUM SYSTEM REQUIREMENTS:

For Macintosh:
Power Macintosh; Mac OS 8.5 or higher; 4 MB Application RAM; 8x Multi-Session CD-ROM drive

For Windows:
Pentium, Celeron or equivalent processor; Windows 95, 98, ME, NT, 2000, XP, Vista; 4 MB Application RAM; 8x Multi-Session CD-ROM drive

28 ITALIAN SONGS AND ARIAS
OF THE 17th AND 18th CENTURIES

Keys in Five Editions

	High Voice	Medium High Voice	Medium Voice	Medium Low Voice	Low Voice
Alma del core	B-flat Major	A Major	F Major	E Major	D Major
Amarilli	A minor	G minor	F-sharp minor	F minor	D minor
Caro mio ben	F Major	E-flat Major	D Major	C Major	B-flat Major
Che fiero costume	A minor	G minor	F minor	E minor*	D minor
Come raggio di sol	G minor	G minor	E minor	D minor	C minor
Danza, danza	C minor	B-flat minor	A minor	G minor	F-sharp minor
Delizie contente	A minor	G minor	F minor	E minor	D minor
Già il sole dal Gange	A Major	A-flat Major	G Major	E-flat Major	D Major
Intorno all'idol mio	F minor	E minor	D minor	C minor	B minor
Lasciatemi morire!	G minor	F minor	E minor	C minor	B minor
Le violette	C Major	B-flat Major	A-flat Major	G Major*	E-flat Major
Nel cor più non mi sento	G Major	F Major	E Major	E-flat Major	D-flat Major
Nina	G minor	G minor	E minor	D minor	C minor
Non posso disperar	G minor	F minor	E-flat minor	D minor	C minor
O cessate di piagarmi	A minor	G minor	F minor	E minor	D minor
O del mio dolce ardor	F-sharp minor	F minor	E-flat minor	D minor	C minor
O leggiadri occhi belli	C Major	B-flat Major	A-flat Major	G Major	F Major
Per la gloria d'adorarvi	A-flat Major	G Major	E-flat Major	D Major	C Major
Pietà, Signore!	D minor	D minor	B minor	A minor	G minor
Pur dicesti, o bocca bella	F Major	E Major	D Major	C Major	B-flat Major
Quella fiamma che m'accende	B-flat minor	A minor	F minor	E minor	D minor
Se Florindo è fedele	B-flat Major	A-flat Major	G Major	F Major	E-flat Major
Se tu m'ami	A minor	G minor	F minor	E minor	D minor
Sebben, crudele	F minor	E minor	D minor	C minor	B-flat minor
Sento nel core	G minor	F minor	E minor	D minor	C minor
Tu lo sai	F Major	E Major	D Major	C Major	B-flat Major
Vergin, tutt'amor	D minor	C minor	B minor	A minor	G minor
Vittoria, vittoria!	D Major	C Major	B-flat Major	A Major	G Major

*After adding High Voice, Medium Voice and Low Voice editions to the original Medium High Voice and Medium Low Voice editions, this Medium Low key has been changed on revision.